THE IONA (

The Iona Community is an ecu
women seeking new ways of living the Gospel in the world.

The Community sees its first task as being the building of community in a world marked by division, injustice and isolation. Although the historic island of Iona is the Iona Community's place of inspiration and renewal, and the sign through which it has become best-known, it seeks to be faithful to its task in every place of human need, initially in the housing schemes and inner-city areas of Britain, more recently in a diversity of other locations also. To build community it is necessary to be part of the struggle for personal and political peace and justice, to stand alongside the disadvantaged, to work towards increased sharing among the churches, to strive for an integrated understanding of spirituality, and to explore ways of celebrating the good news of the Gospel and the unity and dignity of all God's people.

We believe that community is an integral part of Christianity. The Christian faith is incarnational — it begins with the Word made flesh. God's becoming human in the person of Jesus Christ reveals God's loving concern with the whole of human life. Thus it is not possible to make divisions between the spiritual and the material; or, to put it another way, we cannot separate prayer from involvement in the world, and we cannot separate our worship from the way we live our lives. To follow Jesus Christ means giving our whole lives, body, mind and spirit, and not setting aside a special part marked 'religion'. So members of the Iona Community, as part of the church of Jesus Christ, are committed to an obedience to him in which prayer and political action to change the world into a more just place are equally important.

The Community has just over 200 members, who live in different parts of the world, mostly in Britain, but also in Africa, Sri Lanka, New Zealand, Australia, Israel and America. Many types of occupation are represented within the membership, with the biggest single group (just under half) in ordained ministry. From 1969 membership has been open to women, and there are now almost 90 women members. Members share a common discipline in the keeping of which they are mutually account-able — a five-fold rule of daily prayer and Bible study, eco-nomic sharing, planning the use of time, meeting together, and working for peace and justice.

The Community maintains three centres on Iona and Mull: Iona Abbey and the MacLeod Centre on Iona, and Camas Ad-venture Camp on the Ross of Mull. Its administrative headquar-ters are in Community House, Govan, in Glasgow, where it also supports work with young people, the Wild Goose Wor-ship and Resource Groups, and a publishing house, Wild Goose Publications. It publishes a bi-monthly magazine, *Coracle*.

The Community comes under the auspices of the Church of Scotland, through a Board on which other churches are also represented, reflecting the fact that members are drawn from many Christian denominations, Protestant and Roman Catho-lic. It was founded in 1938 by Rev. Dr George F. MacLeod (later Lord MacLeod of Fuinary) who was appalled by the church's lack of impact in working-class communities at a time of high unemployment. He and his colleagues, ministers and craftsmen, joined by many volunteer workers, rebuilt the ruined Abbey buildings of Iona as a sign of the necessary integration of work and worship, of prayer and politics. The rebuilding was com-pleted in 1967. (The Abbey church, passed by the Duke of Ar-gyll to a group of trustees in 1899, had already been restored in 1910.)

The history of the Iona Community

'Only a demanding common task builds community.'
(George MacLeod)

Iona is the home of the Iona Community, but not its place of origin. Its birthplace was in industrial Clydeside, in Govan, the dock area of Glasgow.

George MacLeod, the founder and first leader of the Iona Community, was the minister of Govan Old Parish Church in the early years of the Depression, the 'hungry thirties'. In those years, when most of the men in Govan were unemployed, the church in Govan did pioneer work. Here, people said, was a successful church. Its services were crowded. It was active in local affairs. Then to the surprise of many, George MacLeod resigned his charge. He did so because he felt that the conventional work of the church, however outwardly successful, was not meeting the real needs of people, certainly not the needs of unemployed industrial workers in Govan. Only by experiments in new ways of life and work could the church find the way to make faith live for people in a new industrial age. In particular, two groups of people had to be brought together — industrial workers and ministers.

George MacLeod believed that ministers would understand little of working people until the ways of training clergy were changed. That is why in 1938 he set off to Iona with half a dozen craftsmen and half a dozen young ministers to rebuild the ruined living quarters of Iona Abbey.

Many people thought that George MacLeod must be mad — to leave a successful parish and to go to a remote, inaccessible little island. But his dream was to rebuild on Iona as a sign — a visible, tangible sign of restoration and hope in dark times, a sign of the unity of worship and work, church and industry, spiritual and material.

The contemporary situation was not just one of unemployment, but one of war. Yet slowly the building went on, stone by stone, prayer by prayer. The craftsmen challenged the clergy about the language of their services and about how little they knew about industry; the ministers challenged the craftsmen about prayer. And in living together, they learned that Christian community was no easy thing.

Thus, against a background of unemployment, war, and the breakdown of urban life, the Iona Community was born. Yet the Word had to be made flesh, not just in a building on a beautiful island, but in the ruined cities of Scotland. So after the summers on Iona, the men went back to the mainland.

The ministers were sent in pairs to work in housing schemes, to experiment with different patterns of Christian life. New methods of parish and industrial mission were tried. Iona was never seen as a permanent residence but, as in Columban times, a place where mission started.

Miraculously money for the rebuilding came in steadily. During the war a cargo of wood — just the right size for the dormitory roof — floated onto a nearby beach. People, particularly young people, made pilgrimages to the island, and to respond to this challenge, the Community started youth camps on Iona.

And on the mainland, Community House in Clyde Street, Glasgow played a large part in the development of youth and community work in the west of Scotland, with a range of new activities, for instance in drama and film, education and politics, and the provision of social services. In 1951 controversy over the growing Community within the life of the church ended when the General Assembly of the Church of Scotland unanimously resolved to 'bring the Iona Community within the organisation and jurisdiction of the church, and to integrate it with the life of the church', and appointed the Iona Community Board to liaise officially with the Community.

As the movement grew, more and more people wanted to be associated with it. Categories of Associate members and Friends evolved, and there are now approximately 1400 Associates and 1600 Friends.

The rebuilding was completed in 1967. The life of the Iona Community itself changed, as women were admitted to full membership (from 1969), and as a greater number of lay people joined. The ecumenical composition of the Community has also broadened increasingly over recent years. There are now members from many traditions, including Presbyterian, Anglican, Roman Catholic, Scottish Episcopal, Methodist, United Reformed, Baptist, Quaker and Brethren.

George MacLeod, now the Very Rev. Lord MacLeod of Fuinary, relinquished the leadership of the Community in 1967 and died in 1991, aged 96. He was succeeded by Rev. Ian Reid, who was followed in turn in 1974 by Rev. Graeme Brown, in 1982 by Rev. Ron Ferguson, in 1988 by Rev. John Harvey, and in 1995 by Rev. Norman Shanks.

Why Iona?

Why should a modern community seeking to discover new and relevant ways of relating the Gospel to living in the world decide to be associated with a small and seemingly remote island? There are three main reasons.

First of all, Iona has a most important place in the history of Scotland and of western Christianity. It was to Iona that St Columba, an Irish monk, and member of the royal house of Ireland, came in 563AD to establish a monastic settlement, and to bring Christian faith to the west, and thence to the north, of Scotland, the north of England, and eventually far beyond. The Columban settlement became one of the leading centres of Christian mission in Europe, and monks from Iona went out to evangelise the Scots of Dalriada (Argyll), the Picts of northern Scotland, the Britons of north-east England, and on into Europe, penetrating as far as north Germany and Russia. As part of the Celtic church, and maintaining close links with Ireland, the monks of Iona had a dynamic, robust spirituality, which combined a profound mysticism and sense of the goodness and beauty of creation with an earthy realism. Perhaps these two strands are demonstrated best in the two things which, along with their missionary activity, characterised their life on Iona: the agriculture and fishing by which they lived, and in which they displayed considerable expertise; and their work of illuminating and copying sacred manuscripts, for which they were renowned. The Book of Kells, one of the world's most famous illuminated manuscripts, was probably begun on Iona.

This period of great influence for the Columban settlement came to an end in the ninth century, when, following a series of Viking raids in which many of the monks were killed, they returned to Ireland, taking with them the remains of their founder, St Columba, and their illuminated manuscripts.

After their subsequent return to Iona, the great standing Celtic crosses, of which there were as many as a hundred at one time, were built. St Martin's Cross, which still stands in front of the Abbey, is nearly 1000 years old. Many Scottish kings — possibly including Duncan and Macbeth — were brought to Iona for burial.

The Celtic church gradually was absorbed into the mainstream of western Christianity, which now looked to Rome for leadership, and in the late twelfth century Reginald, Lord of the Isles, invited the Benedictine order to come to Iona. They built the Abbey, which is the foundation of the present-day building, on the site of the Columban settlement. Work began at the beginning of the thirteenth century, and the building was extended and enlarged over the years to include all the usual domestic accommodation of a medieval monastery — cloister, dormitory, refectory, chapter-house, and so on, and a number of smaller chapels. The Benedictines were not a missionary order like the Columban monks. Their life was one of prayer, contemplation and hospitality, and they observed the canonical hours, rising in the night to pray, and continuing throughout the day in a series of nine liturgies. A Benedictine order for women was established in the Nunnery in the village, giving way to an order of Augustinian canonesses. The Benedictines enjoyed nothing like the same influence as the monks of Columba, and their foremost memorial is in the beautiful Abbey buildings.

Round about the time of the Reformation in the sixteenth century, the Abbey gradually fell into disuse, to be rediscovered in the eighteenth and nineteenth centuries by scholars and historians, concerned with the disrepair of this important historical and religious site. Some preservation work was carried out in the nineteenth century, until in 1899 the eighth Duke of Argyll, into whose ownership the island and Abbey had passed, gave the Abbey, the Reilig Oran (graveyard) and the Nunnery to an independent trust, composed of Church of Scotland representatives and representatives of the four ancient Scottish universities. He gave it on condition that the Abbey church be restored as a place of public worship, not for Christians of any one denomination, but for Christians of every tradition — a farsighted ecumenical gesture for that time. By 1910 the Abbey church had been restored, but the living quarters were still in ruins.

Therefore, the second good reason for coming to Iona was that there was a clear task to be accomplished. It was a task that had meaning for the craftsmen, for the ministers, and for the volunteer workers who shared in the rebuilding of the ancient Abbey. They believed that the restoration would act as a hopeful sign for the church and for the world.

Finally, there remains the spirit of the place, of Iona itself. God is present everywhere, and can be sought and encountered even, and perhaps especially vividly, in the places of greatest need. But there are also some places which in their clarity and peace render people particularly open to encounter with God, where the veil which separates the earth and the Kingdom seems tissue-thin. Iona has been such a place for countless generations of pilgrims.

And the very remoteness of this little island, with its spirit and its history, reinforced the serious intent of those who sought to build life together.

THE RULE AND CONCERNS OF THE COMMUNITY

'How good and how lovely it is to live together in unity.'
(Psalm 133: from the morning service of Iona Abbey)

The Iona Community was founded in the belief that we cannot be Christians alone. We need the community of fellow Christians. That, of course, is what the church is about; it is the Body of Christ on earth. But within that body Christians are called into different forms of community. The family is one such form into which most Christians are called. The local congregation or parish is another. Most members of the Iona Community are part of such communities. Historically many Christians have felt themselves called into community in many ways, and to respond to many needs. In its own particular context the Iona Community came into being and continues to exist.

Present-day members are not attempting to be latter-day Benedictines or Columban monks. They take no vow of celibacy, and most are married. Their commitment is not entered into for life (although many have been members for most of their adult lives). Instead they renew their vows year by year, and are free to leave at any time. In no sense have members withdrawn from everyday life — work, family, politics, recreation. Community is not easy, and any romantic notions of the Christian life are soon dispelled within the Iona Community. But members are bound to each other by a common vision of the Gospel task, and by a common discipline of life.

The Rule of the Iona Community

The Iona Community believes that Christian discipleship means living a disciplined life, and that true community demands that we are accountable to one another. Members attempt to live by a five-fold rule, which has evolved over the years. The parts of the rule are:

1) *Prayer and Bible study* — Members undertake to read the Bible regularly and frequently and to pray for each other, for their shared concerns and for the wider work of the church on a daily basis. Thus, using the Community's prayer lectionary Miles Christi, the whole community prays each day of the month for common topics and named members in turn.

2) *Sharing and accounting for the use of money* — Members are under obligation to account to one another for their use of money. They are encouraged to give away and account accordingly for a tithe (10%) of their personal disposable income (that is, gross income less income tax and other statutory allowances and benefits from which are deducted the cost of agreed baseline commitments and expenses arising from special circum-

stances). Of this tithe 6% goes to the wider work of the church and other charitable purposes (members' local congregations, bodies concerned with promoting justice and peace, world development etc.), 2% towards the general work of the Iona Community, 0.5% to particular causes and purposes, including projects in the 'two-thirds world', recommended by members, 1% for purposes decided by the local Family Group, and 0.5% to a fund to cover travel costs for members' attending plenary meetings.

3) *Sharing and accounting for the use of time* — Members are asked to plan, be responsible, and account to one another for their use of time so that proper weighting is given, not simply to work, but equally to leisure and recreation, to time for family, to developing skills or acquiring new ones, to worship and devotion, to voluntary work — and to sleep!

4) *Meeting with and accounting to one another* — Members commit themselves to meet with each other in three plenary gatherings on the mainland and a week in the summer on Iona each year. They also, take part in the working groups and committees which provide advice and decide on the Community's work. Members also meet regularly, usually monthly, in local Family Groups to account to one another for the keeping of the rule and to discuss issues of policy and concern within the Community.

5) *Justice and peace commitment* — Members undertake to work for justice and peace in society at all levels in society. To this end a communal Peace Commitment was unanimously adopted in 1966 and agreed in the following extended form in 1988:

We believe:
- that the Gospel commands us to seek peace founded on justice and that costly reconciliation is at the heart of the Gospel;
- that work for justice, peace and an equitable society is a matter of extreme urgency;

- that God has given us partnership as stewards of creation and that we have a responsibility to live in a right relationship with the whole of God's creation;
- that, handled with integrity, creation can provide for the needs of all, but not for the greed which leads to injustice and inequality, and endangers life on earth;
- that everyone should have the quality and dignity of a full life that requires adequate physical, social and political opportunity, without the oppression of poverty, injustice and fear;
- that social and political action, leading to justice for all people and encouraged by prayer and discussion, is a vital work of the Church at all levels;
- that the use or threatened use of nuclear and other weapons of mass destruction is theologically and morally indefensible and that opposition to their existence is an imperative of the Christian faith.

As members and Family Groups we will:

- engage in forms of political witness and action, prayerfully and thoughtfully, to promote just and peaceful social, political and economic structures;
- work for a British policy of renunciation of all weapons of mass destruction and for the encouragement of other nations, individually or collectively, to do the same;
- work for the establishment of the United Nations Organisation as the principal organ of international reconciliation and security, in place of military alliances;
- support and promote research and education into non-violent ways of achieving justice, peace and a sustainable global society;
- work for reconciliation within and among nations by international sharing and exchange of experience and people, with particular concern for politically and economically oppressed nations.

The Concerns of the Iona Community

The Community has identified seven specific areas of work and witness to focus on through the 1990s. These are: sharing communion by the year 2000; justice, peace, and the integrity of creation; racism and inter-faith matters; the rediscovery of spirituality; the cause of the poor and the exploited; constitutional matters; and work with young people. These reflect both the historical roots of the Community and its understanding of present-day imperatives. We engage in these areas not instead of other Christians (for there are many, many Christians whose witness therein both shames and inspires us), and not in opposition to other Christians (we strongly believe in alliance-building and co-operative ventures, and are often associated with other Christian groups, including local churches, in joint action), but alongside other Christians, challenged, strengthened and supported by them. Increasingly we recognise the practical and prophetic significance of 'networking', and that God's work and the signs of the breaking through of the Kingdom are not limited either to the Community or the wider church, but that there are considerable benefits and opportunities in working also with secular bodies which share our values and objectives.

To facilitate and carry forward its work in these seven areas, the Community has created working groups of members with particular commitment or experience in the area in question. There is no uniform pattern to the size or working arrangements of the various groups. Their approaches depend partly on their composition, partly on the nature and demands of the area to which each relates. In most cases there is an active nucleus which meets regularly and a wider group of 'corresponding members'; and few members are likely to be able to be active in more than one working group. The working groups inform and influence the work and life of the Community in a variety of ways — through, for example, raising awareness of issues within the Community through plenary meetings or *Coracle* articles; through making recommendations for policy initiatives; through providing advice on matters where the Community may seek to influence church or Government; through input to the Iona programme; through networking with other similarly concerned groups.

Sharing Communion by the Year 2000

The Community's commitment to the ecumenical movement is long-standing: it was largely due to this aspect of the Community's work that George MacLeod was awarded the international Templeton Prize for 'Progress in Religion' in 1989; and the Community has been formally associated and closely involved with the new ecumenical structures (Council of Churches for Britain and Ireland, Action of Churches Together in Scotland, Churches Together in England) since shortly after they were created in 1990.

Following ecumenical gatherings on Iona in 1993 and 1995 that recognised much common ground between the churches and expressed the belief that continuing movement towards unity is vital in a world of rapid change, a petition 'Call for 2000' was launched early in 1996. With the intention of obtaining 2000 plus signatures, and focusing on the significance of the year 2000, and the expected celebrations, the expressed aim is to achieve occasions of eucharistic worship, open to all baptised persons, at established ecumenical centres and designated ecumenical gatherings, as a means of grace on our pilgrimage together.

Justice, Peace, and the Integrity of Creation

The 'cold war' may be over, but wars still rage in many parts of the world, and there is profound concern about a whole range of related issues — the widening gulf between the rich North and the suffering two-thirds world of the South; Britain's continuing reliance on nuclear weapons, not least the development of Trident; our lack of commitment as a nation to overseas aid; the opportunity costs of the expansion of the arms trade; the destruction of the environment wrought by modern life-styles and social and economic priorities; and so much else besides.

As a Community we believe that, if we are to be true to the Gospel of Jesus Christ, we must say 'no' to the arms race and be prepared to give up nuclear weapons uniterally. We must also work for peace, by prayer, protest, study, non-violent demonstration, education, reconciliation, and political action towards a more just world. This means a redistribution of the world's resources in favour of the poor and hungry.

The working group has a four-fold focus on security, non-violence, the environment, and alternative approaches to economics ('the new economics'). The Community is carrying forward its work in this area of concern also through exploring the issue of ethical investment, through its support of the work based at Peace House and the Peace Boat project, through its involvement in the World Court Project and the World Council of Churches' programme to overcome violence, and through strengthening and developing links with other groups active in these fields.

Racism and Inter-Faith Matters

Racism in Britain is institutionalised and condoned through racially divisive immigration laws. As a Community we believe that racism is contrary to Christian teaching and that, in our democratic society, we must speak out against unjust and discriminatory legislation and practices and thus express our solidarity with people of other faiths and cultures. Over recent years there has been an increasing number of measures, both within Britain itself and throughout the countries of the European Union, reflecting a xenophobic and narrow form of ethnic nationalism, to strengthen controls and restrictions on immigrants and asylum-seekers. The working group has been effective in extending awareness of these issues within the Community, and in participating in campaigns against such proposals, which conflict with Christian principles of justice, generosity and hospitality. There is recognition also of the need to build on this experience, and on several successful events in promoting Jewish-Christian dialogue, by extending work in the area of inter-religious relations in which several members of the Community are closely engaged.

Rediscovery of Spirituality

Over recent years there has been a burgeoning interest in Celtic spirituality and indeed in spirituality generally. The Community's concern in this area has to do with both understanding and experience — with exposing the frequent romantic misunderstandings about the nature of Celtic spirituality, and with promoting an approach that sees spirituality not as an exercise in pietistic individualised detachment but rather as a multi-faceted engagement or centredness in the life of the Spirit, with a clear social dimension and expression.

Through material produced by this working group members and Family Groups have been helped to explore their own understanding of spirituality and discuss questions relating to the keeping of the Community's Rule and to their own devotional practice. The level of interest in the work of the group, with its development of the idea of 'reflective activism' as a focus for the Community's energy, clearly demonstrates that the link between spirituality and social and political commitment from a Christian perspective is central to the Community's purpose and continuing life.

The Cause of the Poor and the Exploited

From the outset the Community has had a particular concern for those who are marginalised or discriminated against in any way. For many years this concern was expressed through the commitment of members working in parishes in inner cities and peripheral housing schemes, where there was high incidence of urban deprivation, and through a special interest in relations between the developed countries of the North and the 'two-thirds world' of the South. These priorities still remain high on the Community's agenda, but over recent years the issues have been approached in other ways also, especially in alliance with other groups with similar aims and objectives, for instance Church Action on Poverty. Thus there is a focus on unemployment, disability and health service questions, on empowering and listening to those whose voice is seldom heard. Undergirding all this is a fundamental commitment to social justice and to challenging a value system that is based on the operation of market forces and on the encouragement of a kind of possessive individualism that is contrary to the Gospel.

Constitutional Issues

Over the last few years the Community has taken a special interest in the range of issues that concern the government of Britain — on the grounds that these are entirely appropriate matters to be involved with, raising questions of communal well-being, justice, responsibilities and rights that are central to the Gospel. This has led to participation in a number of the initiatives that have evolved relating to the Scottish constitutional issue and the emergence of a new kind of 'civil society', founded on the co-operation of a broad cross-section of organisations, through, for example, the Scottish Constitutional Convention, the Coalition for Scottish Democracy, and the Scottish Civic Assembly. Some attention has also been given to the future direction of the European Union, and the place and contribution of both Scotland and Britain within that, and the significance of other matters of principle such as freedom of information and a Bill of Rights is also recognised.

Work with Young People

For many years work with young people has been one of the major thrusts of the Community. The replacement of the youth camp on Iona by the MacLeod Centre, alongside the continuing work at Camas, on Mull, provide exciting opportunities for work that is both relevant and imaginative. The Community employs a full-time Youth Development Worker who has special responsibility to develop and co-ordinate a programme of events and activities on both Iona and the mainland. Reflecting the importance of this 'area of concern', and seeking to maximise the contribution that young people can make to the continuing life of the Community, the Youth Planning Group provides advice and support for youth activities.

The youth programme on Iona seeks to help young people realise their potential, through finding their own worth and the value in others, and through discovering an expression of Christianity that avoids religiosity and is real and relevant to their own situation. Thus there is a series of events throughout the year for different age groups (students; over 20s; 16-18s; 12-15s), and with different emphases, that aim to bring together people from a range of different social and geographical backgrounds for what is almost inevitably a challenging and rewarding experience. The general aim is to provide an opportunity for sharing and growing together, discovering what is important for young people in a complex and often difficult world. During 'open weeks', outside the peak season, many school and youth groups use the Iona centres, and the year's programme culminates in the Youth Festival, usually held in July.

On the mainland, in addition to responding to requests for information, resources and personal visits, and to a certain amount of preparatory work that is done with groups prior to their visiting Iona, there are a number of follow-up events and reunions, and a newsletter is published, enabling young people to stay in touch with one another and build on and develop the insights and experiences they had on Iona. Recently there has been growing evidence among young people of a desire to express formally their commitment to the life and concerns of the Community, and the category of 'Youth Associates' of the Community has been introduced, with increased participation by young people in developing plans and programmes for exploring concerns of spirituality and social justice, and strengthening and deepening their links with the Community.

Worship

Worship lies at the heart of all the Community's life and concerns. Whenever members gather, in Family Groups or Plenary Meetings, they worship together. The daily life on Iona begins and ends with worship. The work of the Wild Goose Resource Group and the Wild Goose Worship Group is significant within the life of the Community and has made a remarkable contribution to the renewal of worship, through the discovery of new and relevant approaches, and through the production of songs and other resources for liturgy, throughout Britain and beyond.

In worship we celebrate the love of God, and we celebrate our own life together as a gift of God. We seek to discover new ways through which worship may come alive, and a new understanding of God. We are committed to an approach to worship that is *incarnational* — expressing the belief that there is no part of our life that is beyond the reach of our faith; that is *historical* — drawing on the Christian heritage and the experience and creativity of our forebears in the faith; that is *ecumenical* — reflecting the gifts to be received as part of the worldwide church and from the various traditions represented in our membership; that is *creaturely* — allowing response through senses, as well as intellect, and giving full scope for the changing power of prayer; and that is *inclusive* — affirming God's welcome to all who seek to worship in spirit and in truth, irrespective of gender, race, culture, age or education. Above all we are committed to an approach to worship that is thoroughly participative, affirming and sharing individual gifts and corporate resources, recognising that we need God, we need each other, and God needs us, for we are part of the Body, God's hands, eyes, feet in today's world, as St Teresa's famous prayer puts it.

THE ISLANDS WORK OF THE COMMUNITY

'A sanctuary and a light'
(from the prayer of the Iona Community)

Iona Abbey, the MacLeod Centre, and Camas Adventure Centre on Mull, all offer those who participate, for however long or short a time, a unique experience.

Abbey

Within the rebuilt walls of an ancient abbey, whose foundations date back to Benedictine times and whose origins are Celtic, a community life continues which includes and welcomes those who come to work for a year or more, sharing facilities, meals and worship, those who join them for shorter periods as voluntary summer staff, and those who come to stay for a week or so, along with day visitors to the island. It is no coincidence that this community life takes place in a setting with Celtic and Benedictine roots. Both of these traditions emphasised the sacredness of everyday life and asserted that worship and daily life and work were all part and parcel of each other. There was no realm of human activity which was outside the reach of the Gospel message. People, and their lives, were not to be divided into 'spiritual' and 'secular'.

From this, the Iona Community and its island staff stand by a belief that all people are lovable and all human activity capable of redemption. In other words we see good and evil at work throughout life — from personal relationships to international politics — and we can make a decision to be involved in God's kingdom-work, in changing things for the better, in bringing about good where evil prevails, in promoting good where it is breaking through.

The community of resident staff who live in the Abbey all year round tries (and often fails, but tries again) to work out ways of living together where resources are shared, where people are valued and listened to, where people can trust and love one another through their differences. The Warden, who is invariably a member of the Iona Community, is in overall charge, with other members of the long-term resident staff dealing with particular areas (such as programme, maintenance, domestic responsibilities, management of the shop, staff co-ordination) and some coming for a shorter period of around a year to work in posts such as cook, housekeeper, musician, receptionist. Those who join as voluntary staff, in ancillary positions, spend at least seven weeks on the island, sharing in this way of living and working, and for many residents and voluntary staff, the experience affects them so profoundly that they cannot go back to an old way of life without wanting in turn to change that way of living in some way.

Apart from the short closed period (usually in January and February) every week throughout the year the resident group is joined by guests who have come for an informal stay or to join one of the set programmes which are run from March to October. It is here that the words 'only a demanding common task builds community', from a prayer of George MacLeod, take on a special significance. Many guests have had an experience, common to all too many people in today's world, of being buffeted, rejected and hurt to the point of becoming closed and defensive. The Abbey can accommodate 48 people where the community aims to provide a place in which people can feel safe — a sanctuary, where they can open out, talk about their fears, reflect on their lives through a distinctive style of worship, share work and celebration, and join in discussion about the theme for the week, in which contemporary issues are looked at in the light of the Gospel.

Community life — the life of the people who form each particular week's Abbey community — grows fast as people wash dishes together, share in worship planning, arts, music, crafts and drama, enjoy social events together, like the weekly ceilidh and concert. It develops even more so as they chat at the dinner table, in the common room, in odd corners around the building, on walks and on the weekly pilgrimage — a five-hour walk around the island with stops for a brief act of worship at various places of significance, on which they will be joined by those staying in the MacLeod Centre, along with some from hotels and cottages on the island, and by some day visitors. This is the essence of the sanctuary — a place to feel loved, where you are valued for yourself and where your talents are welcome and useful — and if you thought you didn't have any, a place to discover that you have!

And what about the light? The familiar prayer 'Seek for more light ... and follow the light you see' echoes the need to continue on our life's journey in the way we can, but always open to new directions. In Iona Abbey the light comes from surprising places. It may be in formal worship or in the programme discussions that new ideas and the sense of new possibilities are experienced; it may be in talking to a member of staff or to a guest who comes from somewhere on the other side of the island. Down the centuries Iona has been felt to be a special place, a blend of ancient and modern, where people's lives have been touched and transformed in a host of surprising ways, where there can be a strong sense of a 'tissue-thin' closeness to God.

Although day visitors are often on the island for as little as two hours, many of them experience this atmosphere, through exploring the buildings, finding exhibitions about current issues, attending the short Peace and Justice worship each afternoon. And many return for a longer time to join the living community in the Abbey. Even those who do not come back tend to remember the visit for the rest of their lives.

MacLeod Centre

The MacLeod Centre, named after the Community's Founder, was opened by Mrs Leah Tutu in August 1988, during the week of celebrations to mark the Community's fiftieth anniversary. It occupies the site of the former youth camp, the buildings of which (the original huts which those working on the rebuilding of the Abbey had used in the early days of the Community) had reached a state beyond repair.

The 'Mac', as it has come to be known, is built to an attractive vernacular design that was the outcome of an architectural competition and was completed following a successful £1m appeal, that involved both grants from public bodies and a massive fund-raising effort throughout the Community's constituency. It accommodates 52 people, mostly in spacious four to six bedded rooms, and offers a relaxed atmosphere for individuals and families alike, with its safe play areas, its large community room (used for discussion, concerts and ceilidhs), and its well-stocked craft room. Children and young people are especially welcome, and there is a children's programme and several special youth weeks over the summer months. The building has been designed to be accessible to wheelchairs and disabled people in a way that the Abbey cannot be, and provision is made for special dietary needs.

Like the Abbey the 'Mac' seeks to build community week by week among people of differing backgrounds, ages, abilities and outlooks, providing opportunities for both relaxation and the sharing of insights, challenge and hope with friends old and new. Although the 'Mac' is closed for longer over the winter and its programme week by week has different emphases from the Abbey one, the daily routine follows broadly similar lines to the Abbey's, with some sessions, meals and chores arranged separately in each centre, and other shared occasions when guests and staff from both centres come together for worship, social events and other purposes. The two centres thus complement one another and the opening of the 'Mac' has extended the scope for enjoying the Iona experience.

Camas

A very different experience is on offer in a stone-built former salmon-fishing station at Camas on Mull, about three miles from Iona. The centre is run by a team leader, assisted by staff with specialist skills and volunteers. Young people from cities and elsewhere come to Camas for an adventure holiday, usually with canoeing, walking, orienteering, and the excitement of a night sleeping in a cave if the weather is right. Other groups and individuals come to explore issues, build relationships, develop new interests, and face new challenges in this unique setting. Camas has no electricity and the nearest road is twenty minutes' walk over the moor. Here people can really learn about getting along together in a demanding situation that is far removed from their normal environment, and discover that self-reliance and mutual dependence are two sides of the same coin.

Abbey Shop

People who come to Iona even for a few hours are expecting to find out why anybody should bother to rebuild and inhabit a Christian community amid ancient ruins on a remote island — and in the shop they will find plenty of clues. In the book section they will find ample material on Celtic and Scottish history which make the modern relevance of Iona clear, as well as a wide-ranging selection of the most recent books by Christian and other writers who have tried to face up to the most pressing of contemporary problems. There is a stock of good children's books, and pamphlets, tapes, records and song-books connected with the work of the Iona Community. The shop also sells post-cards and posters, tee-shirts and other goods with an Iona theme, as well as hand-made crafts from all over Scotland. The shop is open from 10am to 4pm every weekday and for a short time on Sundays.

Coffee House

As well as books and gifts, visitors are often looking for somewhere to have a cup of tea or a light lunch. The friendly and colourful Coffee House, across the road from the Abbey, provides a welcome every weekday from 10.30am till 4.30pm. All the baking and soups are home-made and relatively inexpensive, and the Coffee House walls also display exhibitions related to the Community's concerns. Each week, during its closed time, the Coffee House is used for several staff gatherings, for both business and leisure purposes, and on occasions it provides a venue for evening events where people can relax and listen to some of the variety of singers and musicians who pass through Iona during the summer months.

Healing Ministry

To be free to live our lives fully and openly, we need to be assured of our wholeness and this often means overcoming barriers of self-loathing, fear and defensiveness, as well as admitting that we cannot do this on our own. In its commitment to the ministry of healing the Iona Community follows Christ's command to be a healing church, and looks not for bodily healing alone, or 'miracle cures', but instead expresses through the various parts of this ministry the mutual support and healing which, as people who live in a broken world and are ourselves invariably broken in some way or other, we all need on our journey through life, rough or smooth.

A circle of intercessors, living all over the world and co-ordinated by the prayer circle secretary, who is a member of the Abbey resident staff, pray regularly for people in particular need of prayer, and every Tuesday, during the Abbey evening service, prayers are offered for particular people and situations, as requested, and the laying on of hands is offered — a corporate act of as many as wish to take part. Taking part in the laying on of hands and receiving this ministry are not mutually exclusive: thus we all express our need for support and our obedience to the command to go forth and heal.

It has always been a central theme of the healing ministry that we should look at the context in which illness and distress occur: so our ministry is as likely to take us into the realms of local and national politics, in an endeavour to change environments and policies which we believe to be responsible for individual illnesses and adversity of all sorts, as it is to be in direct contact with 'sick' people. Nor do we believe that healing is a one-way process; by their demeanour in living in and through their illnesses, even if 'incurable', people who are ill and distressed can often give to others a surer sense of the priorities of life. Healing is about wholeness of people, 'at-one-ment' with themselves, their neighbours, their surroundings, and ultimately with God.

THE MAINLAND WORK OF THE COMMUNITY

'New ways to touch the hearts of all'
(from the prayer of the Iona Community)

The mainland work of the Community is first and foremost what its individual members do in their own situations. There are just over 200 members of the Community. Of these about half are in full-time ministry in parishes, chaplaincies (industrial, hospital and university), theological education, church organisations and the diaconate. Other members are drawn from a wide variety of occupations and interests, which often reflect the concerns of the Community. About twenty work in the field of health — as doctors, in nursing, counselling, pharmacy and administration, and around the same number are engaged in school and university or college teaching. Others are involved with local government and voluntary organisations, in social and community work and other related areas. A number work in industry, some care for families, several are involved in local politics, some are studying and five are on the staff of the Community. Some of the members are not in paid employment, some work part-time, others share jobs, and several are retired. But all share the commitment to pursue the concerns of the Community and put the Rule into practice in whatever is the most appropriate way in their own situation. This individual commitment is the bedrock of the work of the Iona Community, and it is in this we seek to support, encourage and challenge one another. The majority of members live in Scotland, but a significant number are in England, and some live overseas — there are currently six in the United States, two in Africa, and one in Israel, Sri Lanka, Australia, and New Zealand.

Since its inception the Community has been concerned about breaking down the barriers that divide us — between 'working-class' people and the church; between employed and unemployed; between races and nations; between Christianity and other faiths; between 'sick' and 'well'; and more recently between men and women. In seeking to overcome such divisions we are also seeking new ways of rebuilding community — the universal community of justice, love and peace which Christ came to make possible. All our efforts, individually and together, stem from and are primarily concerned with our calling to be servants of Christ and of each other. We hope to be not just a community which stands against injustice, oppression and despair, but also a community which stands for hope, change, and celebration and affirmation of life together. Whether we do this through the existing structures of church and society or by innovative projects, whether by means of local festivals, house churches, demonstrations, co-operatives or the arts, our aim is the renewal of community in the spirit of Jesus Christ.

As well as the initiatives of individual members, the Iona Community has always had a range of mainland projects which reflect its corporate concerns. For many years Community House in Clyde Street, Glasgow served as a significant centre for the provision of educational facilities (including drama and political work) and social services which touched many people's lives. More recently there have been various projects involving, for example, the exploration of work issues, local community outreach, a youth volunteer programme and 'Peregrini' training scheme; and for many years the Community employed a full-time justice and peace worker who, although now working independently, still receives some financial support from the Community towards the running of her resources base — Peace House, near Dunblane. Peace House is one of several 'Columban Houses', which the Community has encouraged — small communities where people who hold the concerns of the Community share a common life, worship together and support each other in the tasks in which they are engaged.

Currently (in the mid 1990s) the Community's corporate mainland outreach is channelled through the activities of the Wild Goose Resource and Worship Groups and the work of the Youth Development Worker, as described above. They are based in Glasgow, at Community House, in the Pearce Institute in Govan, the Community's administrative headquarters along with the Leader of the Community, Norman Shanks, the members of the administrative and financial support staff, and the editor of the *Coracle*, the Community's magazine which is issued six times a year with Community news and articles about the Community's purpose, concerns and activities. The Community's publishing arm, Wild Goose Publications, which produces a range of books, pamphlets, recordings and worship resources reflecting the liturgical, theological and social interests of the Community, is also based in Govan.

Finance and administration

The Iona Community is a registered charity and a company limited by guarantee, with its designated office-bearers and a structure of committees (covering Finance and Staffing, Islands, Mainland, and Publishing, as well as the Council, which is in effect the executive committee) to which members are appointed from the Community's membership at the annual general meeting in the early summer.

The Community is entirely responsible for its own finances. A limited amount, usually on an *ad hoc* rather than a regular basis, comes from grants. Members themselves contribute and covenant part of the money, in accordance with their commitment to the Rule; but the bulk of the funding for the work of the Community comes from its own operations — the shop and coffee house on Iona (the aim is that the Abbey, MacLeod Centre and Camas should be self-supporting rather than profit-making); and fund-raising events such as the annual Daffodil Fair in Glasgow — together with the significant, and much appreciated, amount that comes each year through subscriptions of Associate Members and Friends and donations and legacies from those who are interested in and wish to support the Community's work.

HOW YOU CAN TAKE PART IN THIS MOVEMENT

Our world needs people who are seeking to be obedient to Jesus Christ in their daily lives, people for whom prayer and action to change the world are equally important.

If we are to do it, we need to do it together. In that way we can keep alive the vision, we can support each other, we can be challenged by each other. We need to do it in an ecumenical spirit also — to share closely with people from different traditions, and thus have our lives and understanding enriched.

It is to promote and support such a movement — to find 'new ways to touch the hearts of all' — that the Iona Community exists.

There are several different ways in which it is possible to support and share in the Iona Community's work.

By becoming a Friend of the Iona Community

Friends are those who are interested in the Community's work and concerns and wish simply to stay in touch with and support the Community by their prayers and donations. They receive copies of *Coracle* six times per year. If you are interested in becoming a Friend of the Community, please write to the Membership Secretary, Community House, Pearce Institute, 840 Govan Road, Glasgow G51 3UU.

By becoming an Associate of the Iona Community

Associates are men and women who, because of their agreement with the work and purposes of the Iona Community, wish to commit themselves to a definite participation in the life of the Community. Associates undertake to keep the prayer and Bible study discipline which members observe under the Rule of the Community. There are opportunities for Associates to meet together regularly through regional Associates groups, and in some cases through participation in members' Family Groups; and through the Associates Advisory Group, comprising representatives from different regions of Britain, common interests are explored and dealt with.

Many Associates also keep an economic discipline, contributing, in addition to their annual donation to the work of the Community, a proportion (currently 2%) of their disposable income to a common fund, while others prefer to give a contribution to the fund that is not based on this calculation. The distribution of the Associates common fund, to projects suggested by those participating, is decided annually by the Associates Advisory Group.

Each year Associates receive a copy of Miles Christi, the Community's prayer lectionary, the Associates prayer list, and, every two months, copies of *Coracle*, including Community news and the Iona programme for the year.

On St Columba's Day each year, 9 June, Associates renew their pledge to be associated with the aims, life and work of the Iona Community. They signify this intention by returning a renewal form to the Membership Secretary.

If you are interested in becoming an Associate of the Community, please write to the Membership Secretary, Community House, Pearce Institute, 840 Govan Road, Glasgow G51 3UU.

By becoming a Member of the Iona Community

Members, after a two-year joining programme, commit themselves to keep the five-fold Rule of the Community. The joining programme involves:

- three gatherings in the autumn and spring of the two years, for the purpose of exploring the Rule, concerns and work of the Community, to explore what membership involves, and to enable the new members to get to know one another;
- two weeks in the summer of each year at Camas, for a work week, and on Iona for Community Week;
- a mainland project relating to the concerns of the Community;
- full participation from the outset in local Family Groups and plenary meetings of the Community.

Those who apply for full membership are expected already to be Associate members of the Community, thus ensuring a familiarity with the work and aims of the Community and experience of keeping part of the Rule. Applicants are interviewed before being accepted by the Council of the Community for admission to the new members' programme.

Anyone considering full membership of the Community is asked to write to the Leader, Norman Shanks at Community House, Pearce Institute, 840 Govan Road, Glasgow G51 3UU.

By working as a member of staff of the Iona Community

Each year there are opportunities for people to work at the Abbey and MacLeod Centre on Iona, and at Camas on Mull. Members of resident staff, along with the volunteers, provide hospitality and programmes for the guests who come to the centres each week, and share a common life of work and worship (with a little time for relaxation). This is very demanding work, but it is also immensely enriching. There are about twelve resident staff posts for a period of three years, another twelve or so for one year, and more than twenty volunteer positions for shorter periods from seven weeks to three months. Anyone interested should contact the Staff Co-ordinator, Iona Abbey, Isle of Iona, Argyll PA76 6SN.

In addition vacancies occur from time to time, normally requiring specialist skills, in the Community's office in Glasgow. These are advertised in the *Coracle* and through the press.

A prayer for our own reshaping

O Christ, the master carpenter,
who at the last through wood and nails
purchased our whole salvation,
wield well your tools in the workshop of your world,
so that we who come rough-hewn to your bench
may here be fashioned to a truer beauty of your hand.
We ask it for your own name's sake.
Amen

Recommended further reading

George MacLeod, *We Shall Rebuild* (Iona Community, 1940)
George MacLeod, *Only One Way Left* (Iona Community, 1955)
Ralph Morton, *The Household of Faith* (Iona Community, 1951)
Ralph Morton, *The Twelve together* (Iona Community, 1956)
Ralph Morton, *The Iona Community: personal impressions of the early years* (St Andrew Press, 1970)
Ron Ferguson, *Chasing the Wild Goose* (Fount, 1988)
Ron Ferguson, *George MacLeod* (Collins, 1990)
Ron Ferguson, *Daily Readings from George MacLeod* (Fount, 1991)
John Harvey, *Bridging the Gap* (St Andrew Press, 1987)
Foundation Documents of the Iona Community (first three editions of the *Coracle*, 1938)

Some of the above are out of print but are obtainable through libraries.
See also the catalogue for Wild Goose Publications, which includes a number of books by members of the Community and relating to the Community's concerns.

Titles available from Wild Goose Publications

Song books with full music (titles marked * have companion cassettes)
THE COURAGE TO SAY NO, Songs for Lent and Easter* John Bell and
    Graham Maule
GOD NEVER SLEEPS – PACK OF 12 OCTAVOS* John Bell (guest conductor)
COME ALL YOU PEOPLE, Shorter Songs for Worship* John Bell
PSALMS OF PATIENCE, PROTEST AND PRAISE* John Bell
HEAVEN SHALL NOT WAIT (Wild Goose Songs Vol.1)* John Bell and
    Graham Maule
ENEMY OF APATHY (Wild Goose Songs Vol.2) John Bell and Graham Maule
LOVE FROM BELOW (Wild Goose Songs Vol.3)* John Bell and Graham Maule
INNKEEPERS & LIGHT SLEEPERS* (for Christmas) John Bell
MANY & GREAT (Songs of the World Church Vol.1)* John Bell (ed./arr.)
SENT BY THE LORD (Songs of the World Church Vol.2)* John Bell (ed./arr.)
FREEDOM IS COMING* Anders Nyberg (ed.)
PRAISING A MYSTERY, Brian Wren
BRING MANY NAMES, Brian Wren

CASSETTES & CDs (titles marked † have companion song books)
Tape, THE COURAGE TO SAY NO, Songs for Lent and Easter† Wild Goose
    Worship Group
Tape, GOD NEVER SLEEPS † John Bell (guest conductor)
Tape, COME ALL YOU PEOPLE † Wild Goose Worship Group
CD, PSALMS OF PATIENCE, PROTEST AND PRAISE † Wild Goose
    Worship Group
Tape, PSALMS OF PATIENCE, PROTEST AND PRAISE † Wild Goose
    Worship Group
Tape, HEAVEN SHALL NOT WAIT † Wild Goose Worship Group
Tape, LOVE FROM BELOW † Wild Goose Worship Group
Tape, INNKEEPERS & LIGHT SLEEPERS † (for Christmas) Wild Goose
    Worship Group
Tape, MANY & GREAT † Wild Goose Worship Group
Tape, SENT BY THE LORD † Wild Goose Worship Group
Tape, FREEDOM IS COMING † Fjedur
Tape, TOUCHING PLACE, A, Wild Goose Worship Group
Tape, CLOTH FOR THE CRADLE, Wild Goose Worship Group

DRAMA BOOKS
EH JESUS...YES PETER No. 1, John Bell and Graham Maule
EH JESUS...YES PETER No. 2, John Bell and Graham Maule
EH JESUS...YES PETER No. 3, John Bell and Graham Maule

PRAYER/WORSHIP BOOKS
PATTERN OF OUR DAYS, Liturgies and Resources for Worship,
     (ed.) K. Galloway
PRAYERS AND IDEAS FOR HEALING SERVICES, Ian Cowie
HE WAS IN THE WORLD, Meditations for Public Worship, John Bell
EACH DAY AND EACH NIGHT, Prayers from Iona in the Celtic Tradition,
     Philip Newell
THE IONA COMMUNITY WORSHIP BOOK
WEE WORSHIP BOOK, A, Wild Goose Worship Group
WHOLE EARTH SHALL CRY GLORY, THE, George MacLeod

OTHER BOOKS
EXILE IN ISRAEL: A Personal Journey with the Palestinians, Runa Mackay
FALLEN TO MEDIOCRITY: CALLED TO EXCELLENCE, Erik Cramb
RE-INVENTING THEOLOGY AS THE PEOPLE'S WORK, Ian Fraser